SIA

Henrietta Kraus

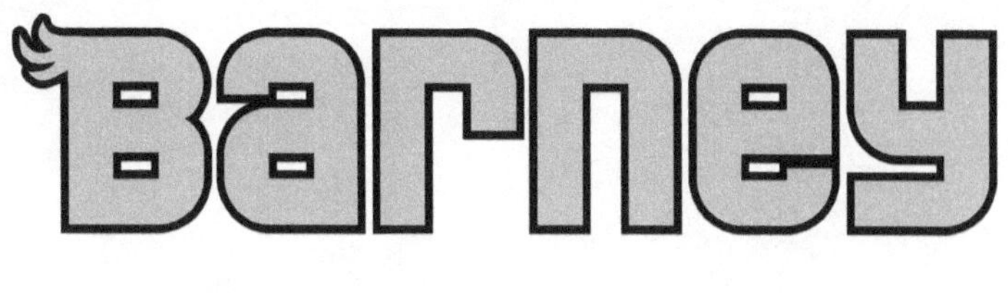

the West Coast Cockatoo

translated by Lara Cantos

SIA Reading Adventure

Henrietta Kraus:
Barney, the West Coast Cockatoo
(SIA Reading Adventure)

ISBN: 978-3-903243-65-1
First edition, 2024

Translation: Lara Cantos
Illustrations: Hedri Widarmawan
Photos: Tim Campbell
Song: Text and music: Lisa Laskey, Recording: Valentina Slobodina
Design and typesetting: Benedikt Maukner
Printing and binding: WIRmachenDRUCK, 71522 Backnang, Germany

Contents

Preface

Dear reader!

This is one of the most touching friendships I have ever come across. A friendship between a human named Tim and a parrot, or rather a cockatoo, named Barney.

They both live on Vancouver Island, Canada, in Tim's house, where Barney was given a wonderful home.

I have rarely come across a more loving friendship between human and animal than that of these two. Tim rescued Barney from an animal shelter and with his love made him one of the happiest birds in the whole world.

Yours,

Henrietta Kraus

Chapter 1

Tim and Barney

The morning rays of sunshine gently caress the stunning natural beauty on Vancouver Island out of its nightly slumber.

Inside a charming house in the middle of a picturesque landscape, in a small town known as Ucluelet, a parrot named Barney stirs and stretches.

Just woken up, Barney reaches out with his beak trying to scratch his right leg – a pricking itch had been bothering him. Next, on to his morning routine.

Barney is wide awake and eagerly awaits his Dad Tim. Barney's cubbyhole is located under the stairs, hence the nickname "Harry

Potter Room", just like the famous sorcerer's apprentice, who also had to sleep under a staircase.

His dad Tim has placed Barney's night cage in this room. Tim's bedroom is right beside it.

Each morning, Tim greets Barney affectionately before going up to the top floor, carrying his little friend on his arm.

On the way up, Barney usually stretches his magnificent wings out in excitement and fidgets with his little head, which Tim likes to call "Barney style".

Barney can do the craziest movements and contortions you have ever seen. And because the parrot is excited to see his dad every day, he performs his tricks on the way up.

In the kitchen, Tim begins preparing Barney's breakfast.

Unlike Tim, who only allows himself a cup of coffee early in the morning, Barney's breakfast is a delicious, substantial meal. It consists of a porridge with frozen dried fruits and vegetables warmed up in the microwave.

The parrot has a small area in the kitchen, his island, where he is spoon-fed by Tim.

Once Barney has finished his tasty meal, his dad hands him a small piece of paper towel so that the parrot can clean his beak.

Then, another day in the life of our two companions can begin!

Chapter 2

A Happy Day

The inquisitive parrot has many toys, which he received as gifts from Tim and from many fans around the world. In fact, Barney is quite famous!

His dad filmed him playing one day and put the video on the internet. Tim hadn't reckoned on the fact that many people saw and liked his clip. And so, he recorded many more videos of Barney and put them on the internet. Thousands and thousands of people all over the world are now fans of the bright parrot and are always happy when they can experience something new with him.

Each new day in Barney's life brings exciting adventures, and his countless friends across the world eagerly follow his exploits. After all, Tim never grows tired of making new videos of Barney.

The same was true on this day: Barney was feeling very playful. His favourite toys are cars. So, Barney grabbed his exciting police toy car and played with it. It even has a blue light, and a siren built in. Tim recorded Barney and uploaded the clip to the internet.

The day just flew by. As he does every evening, Tim put Barney back in his night cage under the stairs. After wishing the parrot good night, Tim went to his bedroom on the upper floor and went to bed.

There is something Tim doesn't know about Barney. Each night, Barney goes on exciting adventures, fantastic journeys and visits fairy tale worlds.

This is Barney's big secret: He can magically bring thoughts to life. The lovable parrot enters fairytale-like, distant worlds where nothing is impossible. Thoughts and wishes immediately become reality.

What this means is that Barney can spend several days travelling in his dream world – while it only takes one night for Tim and everyone else.

Chapter 3

The Adventure Begins

Late one evening, with his great imagination, Barney once again left his cage. By then, Tim had already placed Barney in his "Harry Potter Room" under the stairs and had long since crossed the threshold into the dream world. Unnoticed by Tim, Barney flew out into the starry night.

Tim was fast asleep in his bedroom, while Barney flew higher and higher. He rarely used his wings in his normal everyday life. He preferred using the climbing frames Tim had made for him. But that night, Barney put his wings vigorously to use. Flapping his wings elegantly, he flew higher and higher up into the wide sky.

A glorious moon cast a wondrous beam of light onto the nighttime sea, caressed by a light, cool autumn breeze. Its reflection on the water surface accompanied Barney far below.

A small fishing boat seemed to have strayed onto the sea surface on the Canadian Pacific coast at this late hour, chugging leisurely back to shore. Occasionally, a seagull would cross Barney's flight path in the direction of the nearby sandy beach, Wick Beach, only to dive back into the darkness of night.

Barney thoroughly enjoyed gliding over the rippling waves with his wings spread wide, letting the gentle sea breeze carry him. Every time he started to glide over the water with relish, he thought of Tim's eyes if he were to witness the scene now. As we know, Barney rarely makes use of his wings in Tim's house.

Not far from the small fishing boat, gently bobbing up and down along the cliffs, Barney suddenly heard a sound he had never heard before.

He circled gracefully towards the cliffs and listened more intently. A kind of squeaking or chirping was carried on the waves by the sea breeze from the surface of the water.

Barney paused briefly, pointing his nose down, and began to descend gradually. He wanted to be able to better pick up the trail of that new, previously unknown sound to him.

Moments later, however, he made an intriguing discovery. The water moved considerably more restlessly at the point that seemed to be the starting point of the unknown sound. It was as if the entire surface had lost its natural balance.

Sliding further down, Barney came closer and closer to the mysterious spot. Finally, close enough, he discovered something fascinating: the source of the sound was a small, young dolphin. Full of high spirits, he repeatedly jumped out of the water with full force and in a high arc, only to dive again into the now-shaking water surface, accompanied by excited squeaking sounds.

When the little dolphin emerged the next time, however, he suddenly spotted Barney circling above him.

Abruptly, he slowed down and looked up curiously with shining eyes: "Oh, who are you? At first, I thought you were a seagull!"

He tried to stay upright above the water surface, squeaked again, and then called out an enthusiastic "Good evening!"

Barney resolved to make a soft landing on one of the nearby cliffs. Since he had gotten a few splashes of water from the young dolphin's lively antics, he first fluttered his two wings vigorously and then scrutinized his little friend underwater.

"Well, hi there, little whirlwind! Good evening to you! I don't think I've seen you here before", Barney said.

The dolphin replied, "Hello! My name is Daniel. And you are?"

"I'm Barney. Nice to meet you!"

He returned the greeting with a proud flap of his wings in "Barney style" and looked down at his intrepid new friend with interest.

Skilfully balancing on the water surface, Daniel looked at his new friend: "I've never seen a bird like you before! I've seen countless seagulls around here, but there's something different about you."

Barney laughed out loud.

"Hahahaha! Well, my little friend, maybe that's because I'm not a seagull."

"And if you don't mind me asking, what are you?" Daniel was curious.

Barney lifted his head and replied proudly: "I'm a cockatoo, a member of the parrot family. You seem pretty young to me, little friend, so I don't blame you for not knowing." Barney laughed. Then he asked eagerly: "But tell me, what brings you here at night, so close to land, so close to the cliffs? And what about your parents, aren't they worried?"

"They don't like it when I swim too far away, that's true. As long as they can hear me, they're reassured. As you probably know, we dolphins have excellent hearing!" Daniel replied proudly.

Then he performed an elegant loop, again with a loud beep, in the hope of impressing Barney. He ultimately succeeded in doing so, given his obvious youth.

"What brings me here at night?" Daniel started to answer, "I want to see everything and get to know the world! I would like to know everything about the world, discover everything that is possible for me to explore. Not just the world of water, but also the entire wildlife on land and the world of humans. I've heard sooooo much about it! Barney, I envy your wings! I also want to be able to fly and see everything. The world from your perspective as a bird must be fantastic."

Barney took a long, searching look at his small, excited friend. Then he replied,

"I understand you, little one. Flying is wonderful! But even though I love water, your world under water remains hidden to me."

Barney grinned as he tried again to get rid of an annoying itch under his feathers on his neck with his right leg.

Then he continued: "But apart from that, I imagine diving under water much like flying. There is certainly a great similarity between these two passions."

Barney looked thoughtfully towards the water, while Daniel replied: "Dolphins are mammals, but we have mastered the art of diving brilliantly. And we can hold our breath for several minutes! Just imagine, Barney, two of my family's good friends, a sperm whale and a beaked whale, can even stay under water for up to two hours! I think that's really cool! It means they can dive right down into the deep sea for their prey. We learned all about that at dolphin school."

Daniel dived again, then came up in a high arc, somersaulting directly in front of Barney's eyes as he slid back into the waves with a great splash.

Barney flapped his wings and jumped down onto the nearest rock.

"Listen here, little fellow, show some respect!" Barney was clearly annoyed, "I think I should pay a visit to the Dolphin School to have a little chat about manners and behaviour. Even though I love water, this is unacceptable!" Barney said.

However, Daniel immediately realized from the vibration of his voice that Barney was in no way seriously annoyed. He swam closer to Barney again and flashed him a radiant smile:

"Barney, you really are a friendly, funny guy. The crows I know are rather moody and not very funny. What part of land is home to you, by the way? Tell me, can you tell me something about humans? How close have you come to humans?" Daniel was very curious.

Barney laughed out loud and said, "Tell you about people? I live with a human under the same roof, kid. Or rather, my 'dad' is a human!"

Daniel looked at Barney, studying him. "Barney, I may be very young, but even I know that birds don't have 'human dads'!"

Daniel sounded a little offended, feeling that his new friend was poking fun at him.

"Tim rescued me from an animal shelter in Canada, the 'Grayhaven' ..." Barney gazed thoughtfully into the distance again as he told his story, "After spending ten years in a parrot shelter, I transferred to the Grayhaven for the next two and a half years, where Tim saw me and immediately realized that we were meant for each other. I was, of course, extremely popular amongst the nursing staff there. I am, after all, as you have already noticed, a very amusing and funny chap. The humans love me very much, although at the time I was still quite a crazy bird, a 'wild beast', as Tim sometimes still likes to call me."

Barney laughed loudly, flapped his wings for a moment and looked proudly down at his little new friend again: "You see, Tim is my dad ***and*** also my very best friend. My little one, when I talk about my 'dad', I don't mean my biological father, of course. I have to admit that I can't really remember him very well ..."

Barney scratched his right ear thoughtfully with his left claw. "What I mean to say is that the current dad I live with is my adoptive dad. His name is Tim."

Daniel jumped briefly over a small wave rolling towards him, and then stood bolt upright in front of Barney, splashing around and listening attentively.

Barney continued: "We live together in a human house. I even have my own bedroom in the basement. Since my bedroom is right under the stairs, we named it the 'Harry Potter Room'. I have my sleeping cage there. Tim sleeps very close to me, up the stairs, in his bedroom, not far from the stairs. The living room and kitchen are also upstairs, where my spacious area is located, my 'island' – as we call it. Below that is my wonderful day cage. Tim is truly a great dad! He takes loving care of me and anticipates my every need. You should know that Tim even made special wooden climbing towers for me because I love to climb. My dad, Tim, is a very skilled craftsman, you should see my television climbing tower, it's really cool."

"What is that, a 'television climbing tower', Barney?" Daniel asked curiously. "I know books, and I've also heard of 'Harry Potter', but I've never heard the word 'television' before."

Barney eagerly added: "I wish I could show you some of my phenomenal toys. A young dolphin like you would definitely like them. Even for a 30-year-old parrot like me, they are a fascinating enrichment."

With excitement, Barney bounded up and down on the pointed rock, then flapped his two wings excitedly a few times and continued: "Above all, I would like to show you my countless cars. I got them from my many 'followers' on the internet. They all love me very much and therefore shower me with great gifts!"

Daniel vigorously repeated the question he had asked Barney earlier: "Barney, what is 'television'?"

Daniel immediately went on to say: "Mathilda, a wise old sea turtle I often swim with and have interesting conversations with, is often in our area. She patiently answered my questions and told me a lot about the world on land. The noble old lady has been around for almost 100 years, so she's a walking encyclopedia of land and water. But she's never heard the word 'television', and she's told me a lot about people. I know for a fact that Mathilda has never lived with a human ..."

Lost in thought, Daniel looked over to the mainland and added: "I definitely have to introduce you to Mathilda soon, Barney, and maybe her sister Alma, who is also incredibly likeable and clever. Personally, I'm sure the two of you would get along wonderfully."

Barney explained: "A 'television', my little one, is nothing more than a kind of 'window' to the world for humans. Using a camera, everything that happens outside can be recorded and transmitted to living rooms via a small area that humans call a 'screen'. News, movies, documentaries. Well, even great marine programs about your fabulous underwater world. I have already seen some interesting programs about your sea, so I am already very well-informed about your world. For that, Tim made me my unique television climbing tower. I would love to be able to show it to you. I would very much like to meet your two clever friends, Mathilda and Alma. It would be an honour for me. I am always delighted to meet interesting personalities."

A light wind arose, suddenly causing the waves to crash against the cliffs much more violently. Barney, who hadn't reckoned on that, was startled and flapped his wings nervous: "Heavens! It looks like the weather's going to change!"

The light cast by the moon, which had previously shone unwaveringly on the water surface, was dimmed by a darkening cloud.

"I think a storm is coming, little one." Barney said.

But Daniel enjoyed the big waves, and they even tempted him to do more daring somersaults in the now raging waters. Full of glee and joy, he squeaked.

Barney looked down at Daniel and said, "Even though I love water, my friend, I think I'd better leave now. The weather is getting too unpredictable for me, and I don't feel like getting my wings wet today. Besides, I have to be at my best tomorrow because I'm going to help Tim sort his laundry; tomorrow is wash day."

"What do you mean by 'wash day', Barney?" Daniel wanted to know.

Daniel held himself perfectly still above the water surface, keeping the distance to his new bird friend on the opposite cliff as short as possible, and looked up at him with an incredulous, ironic expression: "I know that humans frequently change their feathers. They call it clothing. I've seen it happening on passing ships and Alma has told me about it, but a parrot bird helps with the laundry? Surely, you're joking, Barney?"

Daniel rolled gleefully up and down on the surface of the water, squeaked a few times, and looked mischievously up at his friend.

"Yes, I do. When Tim sorts the laundry after washing, I carefully fold it with him", Barney couldn't help but chuckle and added, "All right, sometimes I don't help quite so neatly because I might find an exciting sock to play with, but the fact remains: Tim benefits from my 'mental support' as a matter of fact. Just because of my presence."

With a skeptical look, Daniel looked back at Barney and wasn't quite sure whether his new buddy had just told the truth or whether he was just joking and trying to tease him.

Barney ended his explanation with several flaps of his wings and then said goodbye to Daniel: "As I said before, kid, I'll be on my way now. Take care! See you soon! If you come here more often now, we'll definitely see each other again soon. Good night!"

He rose from his ledge and, flapping his wings evenly, went into an elegant climb.

“Good night, Barney! Get home safely! I’m sure we’ll see each other again soon”, Daniel shouted after him.

Then Daniel did a final somersault for the day, waved his tail a few times, causing the water to splash up high, and dove into the dark, night-blue sea. Barney flew into the moonlight, as it glistened on the water.

Chapter 4

Flying Home

Barney had thoroughly enjoyed his flight back home. He couldn't stop thinking about Tim, who would be wide-eyed with amazement if he could see Barney flying so gracefully through the night sky. At home, Barney rarely takes advantage of his big, beautiful wings. Instead, he enjoys exploring his surroundings, checking out interesting things in the living room or on his little island spot in the kitchen. Barney likes to wander around on his two tiny legs, sometimes with a toy, sometimes simply exploring the world around him. When Tim's around, Barney will often hop onto Tim's arm, and Tim will set him down wherever Barney wants, letting him go on his mini adventures within the house.

Although Barney had been a bit wild and energetic at the beginning, which earned him the playful nickname "wild beast", he and Tim are now as close as two friends can be. They share a special bond, like two peas in a pod. However, Barney is still a bit of a mischievous bird. He keeps his nightly activities and adventurous excursions outside the house a well-guarded secret, known only to him.

One evening, Barney stumbled upon a remarkable discovery: he could dream so vividly that it felt like he left his cage, purely through his imagination. The first time it happened, he was startled to find himself standing outside his cage, looking back at his body, fast asleep. It took him a moment to realize what was happening, but soon he got used to this new ability. After all, it allowed him to look at himself from the outside, something he had only ever been able to do before in front of the bathroom mirror.

With his “second body”, Barney could go anywhere he wanted, reaching any place in the world in the blink of an eye. He could even fly freely, as he had just done, without any limits or obstacles. No walls, no closed doors – nothing could stop him. It felt as if he had become weightless, as light as a feather. From outside his sleeping cage, he could see his real body resting peacefully, almost like looking at a reflection in a mirror.

On this night, Barney was making his way back from the sandy shores of Pacific Rim National Park, heading home to Ucluelet. Even though it was nighttime, he could spot Tim’s house from far away. The stars twinkled brightly above, and the moon cast a soft, magical light over the landscape. Barney was flying high in the sky, and from his lofty perch, the houses below looked like miniature toy buildings. As he began to descend, he enjoyed the fresh, cool night air and, the closer he got to the ground, the more he could soak up the delightful smell of the trees and plants. Ucluelet had truly become special to him; the people in this little town on the southern tip of the Esowista Peninsula adored him. He was a small-town celebrity, just as popular here as he might be on Facebook or Instagram.

Now, Barney could see his house clearly, and within seconds, he landed softly on the grass. Barney loved the feel of grass under his tiny feet. He toddled across the yard to the side of the house, where his bedroom – the "Harry Potter Room", as Tim called it – was nestled in the cozy basement. Slipping skilfully through the wall, he flew directly into his cage.

Once back in his roost, Barney felt himself reconnect with his real bird body. He took a quick, refreshing sip of water before settling in comfortably, ready for a few more hours of peaceful sleep.

Chapter 5

A Cozy Day at Home

It felt as if he had only just fallen asleep when the door to the "Harry Potter Room" opened, and Tim stepped over the threshold into the room.

Tim, a tall man with a strong build, always ties his hair neatly into a ponytail. He carefully approached Barney's cage, gently lifting away the blanket that covered it. With a warm smile, he greeted Barney, saying, "Hello, Barney!" As always, Barney, thrilled by the attention, let out a perfect imitation of the telephone ringtone: "Rrrrrriiinnnggg!" Then he stretched out, fluffed up his feathers, and gave himself a quick preen, balancing on his left leg while reaching his beak to his back. To say good morning properly, Barney greeted Tim with a few soft "eye kisses", nuzzling Tim's face with his beak, followed by a little wiggle of his wings in his unique "Barney style".

Barney hopped onto Tim's arm, settling on the back of Tim's hand – his usual mode of morning transport. This routine had become a sweet habit, with Barney often starting the day by giving Tim affectionate eye kisses. The once-rowdy parrot had found a gentle way to show his love for his human companion.

Tim closed the cage door and carried Barney upstairs. They walked up together, passing the bathroom and going straight into the living room, which connected to the kitchen. This was Barney's space, equipped with climbing posts and gymnastics stands just for him. Tim began preparing breakfast for Barney, carefully spooning it onto his special spot on the kitchen island. Barney always loved his breakfast, and when he was finished, Tim handed him a small piece of kitchen paper to clean his beak – very fitting

for a well-mannered, dignified bird like Barney.

After breakfast, Barney climbed down the wooden posts Tim had made for him, toddling on his little feet towards his day cage. Just outside the cage, he found his toy T. rex lying on the floor from the day before. One of his fans had gifted him this toy, and while he'd been a bit cautious of the "scary" creature at first, he had since warmed up to it. Barney picked up his T. rex and delivered it to the back of his cage, his "man cave", as Tim called it. This was his retreat, a special corner for storing his toys.

Barney's thoughts drifted to Daniel, his new friend – a curious little dolphin. He imagined how impressed Daniel would be by his cool T. rex toy. Barney made a mental note to tell Daniel all about dinosaurs and their origins during their next meeting. He was certain that Daniel would find it as exciting and interesting as he did.

After tucking away his T. rex, Barney scratched an itch on his right leg and left the cage again. He remembered he had work to do with Tim today – sorting laundry! He'd proudly shared his laundry expertise with Daniel before, and now he was ready to assist Tim.

Barney scurried across the floor toward the kitchen, where Tim was already folding clothes, stacking them neatly in piles. Barney manoeuvred himself over a chair leg, up the backrest, and finally trotted onto the shelf. With a cheerful "Hello, Barney! Hello, Barney!" he mimicked the friendly greetings he often received from his fans around town. It was his signature greeting, a little catchphrase that brought smiles to everyone who knew him.

As usual, Barney joined in the folding routine, grabbing a piece or two of laundry and helping from a "cockatoo's perspective", which meant his support was mostly mental. During their work, Barney gave Tim a few more eye kisses – a sign of love that always melted Tim's heart, who responded by gently stroking Barney's head.

Suddenly, Barney gave a happy flutter of his wings and, to Tim's surprise, flew a short distance to the work surface across from him. "Whoooaaa, Barney!" Tim exclaimed, ducking down to hide under the worktop before playfully leaping out, shouting, "Peekaboo! Peekaboo!" Barney flinched in delight, instantly recognizing their favourite game. With a playful gleam, Barney dove under a pile of warm, fresh laundry. Tim, delighted, pretended to search for him, adding to the fun. They played like this for a while, laughter, and chirps filling the air, before Barney trotted back toward his toy room.

Over the years, Barney had built up quite a collection in his "pantry of happiness", filled with toys like the T. rex, a plastic telephone, a blue police car, and many more. It was

time to enjoy another round of fun with Tim. Barney grabbed his T. rex and scurried back up to his "man cave", where he noticed one of his Minion toys he had left behind. With a quick decision, he tossed the Minion toy out of the cage in an impressive arc.

"Whooooaaa! Barney!" Tim cheered as the Minion landed in the laundry basket beside the shelf. Laughing, he asked, "What are you up to, Barney?" They shared a moment of playful mischief before the day carried on.

That evening, before bedtime, Tim and Barney relaxed by watching a bit of TV together. When it was time to turn in, Barney returned to his cozy "Harry Potter Room" in his night cage. Tim said goodnight, covering the cage gently before heading up to his room. They both drifted off to sleep, knowing that another day of excitement and fun awaited them in the morning.

Chapter 6

An Exciting Trip to Long Beach

The weather was beautiful that day – the sun was shining bright, and a light breeze drifted through the air. So, Tim and Barney decided to take a little afternoon trip to Long Beach in the Pacific Rim National Park. Barney always loved going outside, especially during the day, when the gentle sea breeze rustled his feathers and new things to explore seemed endless.

As usual, Tim put Barney's orange harness on, carefully slipping the bright ribbon over his wings. Soon they were on their way. It only took about 25 minutes by car to reach Long Beach, one of the largest and longest beaches in the park, stretching along the west coast of Vancouver Island. Constant waves rolling in from the open Pacific Ocean made it a favourite spot for surfers.

People were always happy to see Tim and Barney at the beach. Barney greeted everyone strolling by or relaxing nearby with a cheerful "Hello, Barney!" And many people were just as thrilled to greet him back.

That afternoon, along with passionate surfers, a few furry friends were playing in the sand, sniffing the salty air. One dog named Patricia, a medium-sized dog wearing a red bandana, was especially curious about Barney. As she walked by with her owner, she spotted him. A bird that talked like a human – now that was something unusual! Patricia looked up at him with wide, fascinated eyes, and Barney noticed her, too. He hadn't spent much time around dogs before, but he liked Patricia right away.

Barney wanted to impress her, so he performed his famous "Barney style" dance, twisting his body and making funny noises. Patricia took a few steps back, unsure of

what to make of this odd but charming bird. Barney tried even harder to get her attention by mimicking a phone ringing. Patricia froze and turned back to look at him in awe; she'd never heard a bird make a sound like that!

Tim and Barney had come to relax, while Patricia's family was out surfing, so their paths only crossed for a short time. But it was still an interesting encounter for both of them.

On the car ride home, Barney thought a lot about Patricia. But his thoughts also drifted to his friend, Daniel, and he decided to tell him all about the funny dog he'd met today. Back at home, Tim made Barney a tasty sweet potato dinner, and afterwards, it was time for bed. The day had flown by, but Barney didn't feel sleepy yet.

To Tim's surprise, Barney toddled down the stairs on his own two little feet instead of riding on Tim's arm like he usually did. He made his way to the bathroom, not to enjoy a "wellness shower" under the sink or to nibble on Tim's toothbrush, but to investigate the trash can next to the toilet. Normally, Barney would have gone to his cozy "Harry Potter Room" under the stairs to settle down for the night. But tonight, feeling mischievous, he decided to try tipping over the bathroom trash can. Tim wasn't a fan of Barney's trash-diving habit, but Barney always seemed to find something interesting inside. Despite Tim's many warnings, Barney finally managed to tip the can over with his beak, spilling its contents.

"Barney, bedtime!" Tim called, gently but firmly, as he cleaned up the little mess. He then offered Barney his arm as a "transportation service" back to his sleeping quarters. Once they reached the "Harry Potter Room", Tim carefully opened the door to

Barney's night cage and placed his feathered friend inside.

"Goodnight, Barney", Tim said, giving him a gentle pat on the head before quietly leaving the room.

Barney's next adventure awaited him in his dreams, as he drifted off into a starry night ...

Chapter 7

Fritz, the Seal

Tim had already gone to bed and was drifting off to sleep as the moonlight overtook the room in a soft, yellowish haze. Stars glittered over Vancouver Island, transforming the night into a sparkling wonder. Just as Barney was falling asleep himself, he imagined himself slipping out of his little bird body. Suddenly, he was outside, soaring into the night sky with a gentle flap of his wings.

The air smelled lovely. Barney took a deep breath, inhaling the mingling scents of sea and forest. Every flap of his wings lifted him higher, and soon, the houses in Ucluelet looked like a tiny toy town below.

Barney made his way to Wick Beach, where he'd met his dolphin friend, Daniel, the other night. Pausing midair, he peered down at the moonlit water, its surface shimmering and shifting with the night breeze.

To his excitement, the water beneath seemed alive with movement. Barney decided to investigate, descending with a familiar ringing call to draw attention to himself.

"Oh, for heaven's sake! What is all this racket?" came an irritated voice below. Barney stopped mid-dive, startled. A seal poked his head above water, wrinkling his nose in displeasure.

"What in the world is that dreadful noise?" the seal grumbled.

"Oh! Sorry!" Barney flapped both wings apologetically. "I thought you were my friend."

The seal raised an eyebrow. "A friend? I've never seen a seagull like you around here before."

"Oh, I'm not a seagull! I'm Barney – a Moluccan cockatoo!" Barney said with a laugh, perching on a floating piece of wood near the seal.

"Fascinating", said the seal, sounding skeptical. "My name's Fritz. But what brings a bird like you to these parts, and what's all the fuss about?"

"Nice to meet you, Fritz!" Barney replied and finally sat down on the piece of wood that probably came from a raft. "I live nearby with my dad, Tim, who adopted me from a bird shelter. I've got a wonderful life now, and I like exploring at night. Just last time, I met a new friend here – a young dolphin named Daniel."

At the mention of Daniel, Fritz chuckled. "Daniel? Oh, I know him well! He's the most curious, pesky little dolphin around. Knows how to 'saw' on everyone's nerves with his endless questions."

Just then, a loud "Baaaa!" erupted from Fritz's mouth, startling Barney. He let out an excited "Rrrrrriiiinnnngggg!" in response, imitating his favourite phone ringtone. Fritz wrinkled his nose again in annoyance, but Barney's excitement only grew as the water beside him began to stir. To his delight, Daniel leapt out of the water with a squeal of joy.

"Barney! Fritz! What a surprise!" Daniel said, splashing down beside them.

"Hello, Daniel!" Barney replied happy. "I was looking for you and thought I'd found you!"

"Oh, I recognized Fritz's call from far away! I've got excellent ears, you know," Daniel said.

The three friends chatted, and Daniel proudly explained how Barney lived with his dad, Tim, who had rescued him. Fritz listened thoughtfully, impressed by the bond between Barney and Tim.

Barney told them about the fun he had helping with laundry, the way humans changed their "feather clothes" in bright colours, and even about his new toy fish, a gift from a fan. Daniel was especially fascinated as Barney described their favourite hide-and-seek game, "Peekaboo".

Barney also told them about his day at the beach, where he'd met a friendly dog named Patricia. "She was wearing a red bandana and looked so loyal and curious. I think we'd make a great team!"

"Barney, your life sounds so exciting! I'd love to join you on one of your adventures", Daniel said wistfully.

"Careful, young one", Fritz interrupted with a chuckle. "All that glitters is not gold."

Daniel tilted his head in confusion. "Gold? What do you mean, Fritz?"

"Just remember, things aren't always as they seem. You're lucky, Barney, to have found a friend in Tim, but it's wise to be cautious", Fritz said wisely.

"Very true", Barney nodded. Then, he asked Fritz, "How old are you anyway?"

"Ha! I'm 33 years old, a respectable age for a seal. We seals usually live around 30 years, while walruses live to 40, and eared seals often only to 20. But you, Barney – you're a greenhorn! Moluccan cockatoos can live up to 80 years."

Daniel looked amazed at Barney. "I had no idea you could live so long! That's awesome!"

Barney laughed. "Guess that makes you a greenhorn, too, Daniel!"

Daniel splashed Barney with his tail fin, and Barney leapt off his floating stick in surprise. He fluttered to a nearby rocky hill he hadn't noticed before, landing on its slippery surface and shaking his head in mock annoyance. "Naughty aquatic mammal! Well, the young dolphins nowadays."

But just then, Barney froze, jolted awake by something startling. He glanced around, unsure of what had just happened.

Chapter 8

The Wise Tortoise, Mathilda

Did his new place to sit just budge? Or had it sunk?

"Heavens! What the hell was that?" Barney paused in shock for a brief moment a meter above the water to get his thoughts in order. His two buddies watched the scenario with amusement. In the next second, a melodious voice with an extremely reassuring tone suddenly sounded from the stone. To everyone's great surprise, the head of a turtle suddenly protruded from the water. What Barney had thought was a slippery rock surface turned out to be a handsome sea turtle.

Daniel looked over at Barney, startled. In the next second, he turned his gaze to the large, slippery surface appearing beneath him. With shining eyes, he beeped as loud as he could and shouted: "Mathilda! Guys, it's Mathilda!" The voice was also instantly familiar.

Mathilda stuck her little head as far out of the water as she could and began to curiously scrutinize the interesting characters present.

"Good evening, everyone!" Mathilda greeted the others, "Maybe I'm wrong, but I felt as if I had heard my name before. Am I right about that?"

"We were just talking about you, Mathilda, that's right! About you and your sister Alma. How nice to see you!" Daniel squealed with delight.

"I was just travelling around here, my little one, and as you know, I have good ears", Mathilda replied.

"We talked about age", Daniel explained, "Fritz said that every age should be judged in different ways, namely in relation to how old someone can actually get. For Fritz, his proud 33 years as a seal are already a lot. You and Alma, on the other hand, were still very young when you were as old as Fritz is now."

Mathilda looked at everyone here again with a scrutinizing gaze and finally said: "Am I right in thinking that Fritz is the gracious Seal here? With respect, what a very interesting company here."

Mathilda looked up wide-eyed at Barney, who had now settled back comfortably on his original seat, the floating wooden stick. From there, he listened to the conversation.

"A parrot bird! Well, well, well! Or rather, a cockatoo! Would someone be so kind as to introduce me to the present round of personalities?" asked Mathilda.

"Oh Mathilda, please excuse me! The big surprise of your appearance made me forget my politeness!" Daniel readily introduced his new friends to the noble turtle lady.

First of all, Barney, whom he himself had initially mistakenly assigned to the crow family. He was more than a little surprised that Mathilda had immediately recognized him as a parrot bird. Although not surprising anyway, as wise as his turtle friend was!

Then his new seal friend Fritz, who flattered him by standing up with his whiskers and trying to make himself taller.

"Pleased to meet you all", Mathilda's gaze wandered from face to face, finally lingering on Daniel with a friendly smile.

Mathilda then reported: "Regarding your discussion about age, I would also like to mention the remarkable age of my conspecific Jonathan on the island of St. Helena and that of my conspecific Esmeralda, also a very old lady. Jonathan is currently one of the world's oldest turtles – with a proud 190 years on his shell. This also applies to Esmeralda, who lives on Bird Island in the Seychelles. These are currently the oldest living land animals! Have I missed anything else in the current conversation?"

Fritz, the senior seal, surprisingly spoke up and proudly added: "As well as the 'relativity' of age, I also talked about 'appearance and reality'."

"Oh yes", Daniel remembered, "Fritz wanted to explain something to me about that! Namely, that things or people don't always have to be what they seem at first glance. In this context, he also mentioned Tim, who had rescued Barney, who really is just as likeable as he seemed from the start. But that cannot be taken for granted. Not all people who seem nice really are."

Mathilda listened attentively to Daniel's words and then added: "True, true. People, but also other beings, not to mention objects, can turn out to be different from what they seem at first glance. A clever seal, your friend Fritz."

After a short pause for reflection, Mathilda continued: "The question of 'appearance and reality' is also an important topic in the history of philosophy. And not to forget: Likewise, a thing that at first seems negative can eventually turn out to be positive."

Daniel looked at his old turtle friend with wide eyes: "What exactly are you meaning, Mathilda?"

Barney raised his voice unexpectedly: "A little example, my friend: you want to swim to a beautiful coral reef. On the way, you suffer an injury due to a collision with a fishing hook and are forced to change your route as a result. Naturally, you are very disappointed. On the way back, however, you meet a wonderful dolphin lady with whom you develop a deep friendship that will last a lifetime. But you would never have met her if you hadn't injured yourself and continued your journey as planned."

"Oh, Barney! I think I know what Mathilda means now", Daniel was relieved.

Barney added: "I don't want you to think I'm suggesting that the little mishap with the fishhook is fundamentally a positive thing.

But it's not entirely a negative thing, as it seemed at first."

Mathilda smiled and stretched her neck towards Barney and whispered to him in a soft but insistent voice: "Barney, you explained that beautifully."

In the next moment, she turned her gaze back to Daniel: "Even if this is an entirely different example, there are similar things with people. Your buddy Fritz had already mentioned that: Not every person who appears evil at first glance actually has to be. Often an unpleasant and rather nasty-looking person is in possession of a warmer heart than some people who are exuberantly friendly at first sight. As an aging tortoise, I already have some experience of this ..."

The noble old turtle lady now let her gaze glide thoughtfully over the vast dark expanse of sea, before finally pausing, lost in thought, on the adjacent horizon: "It's such a thing with good and evil … Ever since our planet and all life on it have existed, it's been a constant disaster."

Daniel looked at his friend Mathilda with wide eyes: "Do you think there is good and evil somewhere out there in the universe? Or is that just a problem on our planet Earth?"

Mathilda's gaze lingered on the mighty horizon and, after a moment's thought, she replied: "That's a fair question, my little one …"

"That's enough philosophical ramblings!" Fritz blurted out spontaneously, "Did you hear that?"

"What do you mean, Fritz?" Daniel turned his eyes away from Mathilda and looked at Fritz, startled.

"Hush! Now I hear it, too!" Barney raised his crest in surprise and listened.

Mathilda stretched her neck and then whispered: "Now I can hear it, too, even with my old turtle ears. But what's that strange noise I hear?"

Barney, who was always holding his feathered cap up, pricked up his ears and replied in a whispering voice: "Shush! Do you hear that?"

Everyone listened.

"Well, I can't hear anything, absolutely nothing", Fritz replied with conviction.

"Quiet, Fritz!" Daniel demanded, "Now I hear it, too!"

After a few brisk fin strokes, Daniel paused for a moment to listen carefully.

Chapter 9

Lea and her Furry Friend, Sparko

A soft whimper echoed at regular intervals, interrupted by restless splashes.

"Barney's right!" Mathilda raised her head a little higher to figure out where the noise was coming from.

Barney lifted off from his place and tried to locate the desperate whimpering. He sniffed the air and caught the scent immediately.

He could hardly believe his eyes. The source of the sound was a four-legged friend struggling about half a kilometre away in the water. The dog was fighting to stay afloat, clearly using every last bit of his strength.

"Over here, guys!" Barney shouted, flapping his wings excitedly. He let out his signature call, guiding the others toward him.

Daniel, Fritz, and Mathilda rushed to Barney. As they got closer, they saw a young, desperate Jack Russell terrier frantically trying to keep his head above water.

Mathilda acted quickly, diving under the small dog and lifting him onto her strong shell, supporting his kicking legs. The terrier managed to stand and catch his breath, then shook himself off and, still a bit shaky, started wagging his tail.

"Woof! Woof! Where did you all come from? Thank heavens, you're here! I was nearly out of strength! Thank you so much! My name is Sparko. And who are you all?" said the young dog.

Daniel leaned his beak on Mathilda's shell, looked up at Sparko, and replied, "Hello, I'm Daniel. The lady you're standing on is Mathilda. The flashy parrot who found you is our friend Barney, and the fourth in our group

is Fritz the seal. But tell us, Sparko, how did you end up out here in the ocean all alone?"

Instead of answering, Sparko's tail wagged even faster as he said, "There's no time to lose! We have to find my owner! I'll explain everything later, but my friend Lea fell into the water, too!"

Barney looked at his friends in shock. Without waiting for anyone to say a word, he took off into the sky, searching the area.

And then: There – not too far away, closer to the shore, something dark floated on the water.

Barney hovered for a moment, but the figure was too unclear to make out. He began to descend, and as he got closer, he saw the shape of a young girl floating with her arms wrapped around a wooden plank.

Barney settled beside her and nudged her gently with his beak, hoping to wake her. Nothing.

He tried again, this time using his "eye kisses", softly brushing her eyes with his beak. And just like that, the little girl's eyes fluttered open.

A bit dazed, she brushed a dark strand of hair from her face and looked at Barney in amazement. "Who are you? What happened?!"

Lea rubbed her eyes, then gasped in excitement. "I know you! You're Barney, the funny cockatoo! I've seen you online! My sister Bella and I watch your videos all the time!"

Barney looked astonished, his crest raising slightly.

Lea continued, "You're Tim's Barney! But how did you get here? And why am I floating in the water? And – oh no! Where's Sparko?" She looked around frantically, trying to remember what happened. Slowly, her memory returned.

She had wanted to go outside one last time to see the stars and feel the ocean breeze. Sparko needed a walk anyway, she'd thought. So she had quietly sneaked out of the hotel with him, not wanting to wake her parents, who might not have allowed her to go out so late anyway.

She remembered the strong wind, the waves growing more powerful, and that one big wave that knocked her off balance and pulled her into the water. She had tried to swim back, but each wave pushed her further out. And Sparko had jumped in after her!

Barney, who constantly had his crest raised in amazement, listened attentively to Lea's story.

"Let me guess", Barney said finally. "The water swept you both away and separated you, and you tried to stay afloat until you passed out. We must have arrived just in time! And you're so lucky you had that plank!"

Lea gave Barney a puzzled look. "We?" she asked. "What do you mean, 'we'?"

Just then, a big splash sounded nearby. Out of the water appeared Daniel, flipping through the air and squealing with excitement. He did a somersault, then splashed back down and grinned at Lea.

"Oh my goodness! Who are you?" Lea asked in amazement.

"I'm Daniel! That seal over there is Fritz, and the wise lady carrying Sparko is Mathilda. And you already know Barney", Daniel said, bobbing in the water with a proud grin.

Lea could hardly believe her eyes. She brushed away the water splashed onto her face by Daniel's enthusiastic fin flip and shouted, "Sparko! Sparko!"

In her excitement, she slipped off her wooden plank and landed in front of Mathilda, where her beloved Sparko still lay. A few tears of joy escaped Lea's eyes and joined the waters of the sea.

Chapter 10

Reunited

Sparko barked with joy when he saw Lea. His tail wagged so hard it made his whole body shake with excitement.

"Am I dreaming? My dear Sparko! This is a miracle – you're okay! Thank you!" Lea cried out, wiping away her last tears with the back of her left arm. At the same time, she leaned on Mathilda's left fin for support with her other arm.

Sparko then leaped into the water and landed right in Lea's arms. She hugged him tightly, and Sparko licked her face all over. Both of them were thrilled to finally be back together.

Meanwhile, Barney had cheekily perched himself on Daniel's back and was happily humming a tune. Lea, still holding Sparko close, listened to the melody. It sounded familiar to her.

"Barney, what are you whistling? I know that one!" Lea called.

Instead of answering, Barney suddenly snorted, fluffed his feathers, and flapped his wings. Then he joked, "My feathers are all wet from all this splashing! If only my dad could dry me off with the hairdryer now."

Lea laughed, "Oh, Barney! You're the funniest, coolest bird I know, but I recognize that tune! Tell me, what were you just whistling?"

Everyone's eyes were now on Barney. But Barney didn't answer – he just kept whistling happily.

"Oh my goodness! Now I remember! That's the Barney song! My sister Bella loves that song. We've sung it together so many times. Bella's going to be amazed when I tell her all about this rescue!"

Lea glanced at Daniel, who was also trying to whistle along with the tune. But just then, seal Fritz interrupted them, "Hey, I would rather not be a downer, but shouldn't we get Lea and Sparko back to shore? Her parents must be really worried!"

Mathilda nodded her wise old head. "You're absolutely right, Mr. Fritz. We need to get them to shore right away."

Barney agreed, too. "Let's head back. A few hours of sleep would do me good right now. Tim and I are leaving early tomorrow to catch the ferry because we're going to visit Grandma!"

"How exciting, Barney! You're taking the ferry to Vancouver! We'll have to meet up again while I'm here with my parents. You'll have to tell me all about your adventures with your grandma. Promise, Barney?"

Lea's face was glowing. Even after everything that had happened, she could barely hold in her excitement. Barney flapped his wings and replied, "Promise, Lea. It's a deal!"

Mathilda dove underwater, carrying Lea and Sparko on her back as they headed toward the shore. Daniel led the way with Barney perched on his back, followed by Fritz the seal.

They all set off for the shore together, with Barney whistling his tune happily and Lea singing the words with pride. Daniel beeped to the rhythm, and Fritz and Sparko joined in enthusiastically.

The Barney Song

Music and lyrics: Lisa Laskey

9
whistle a tune and dance for you, Bar-ney the Cock - a - too! He's cute, he's smart, he'll melt your heart,
loves to say "I was shot! I was shot!" He'll eat his grapes and take a bath,
C F G7 C C
12
Bar-ney the Cock - a - too! He loves to take his cars ap-part, Bar-ney the Cock - a - too!
Some - day he'll say "I love you, dad!"
F G7 C C F G7 C

15
Whistle
Hel - lo Bar-ney, the West-coast Cock - a - too! Hel - lo Bar-ney, Bar - ney we love you!
F C G Am F C G C
19
Whistle
D.S. al Coda
Bar - ney we love you! Bar - ney we love you!
Some
C Dm/F C/G G Am C Dm/F C/G G C

23
Hel - lo Bar-ney, the West - coast Cock - a - too! Hel - lo Bar-ney,
F C G Am F C
26
1.
Bar - ney we love you!
G C
2.
Bar - ney we love you!
G C C
Whistle

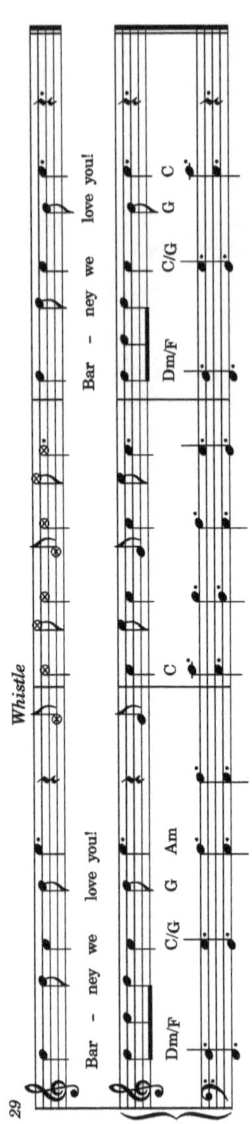
29
Whistle
Bar - ney we love you!
Dm/F C/G G Am
C
Bar - ney we love you!
Dm/F C/G G C

You can download and listen to the song here:

https://sia.education/s/374163

These kids sang the song for the recording together with the musician Viktoria Slobodina:

- Lydia (11 years old)
- Anna Maria (9 years old)
- Valentina (11 years old)
- Maya (9 years old)
- Mariia (10 years old)
- Miron (12 years old)
- Asal (13 years old)

Check Out Barney on Social Media

Instagram:

https://www.instagram.com/barney_the_west_coast_cockatoo

Facebook

https://www.facebook.com/westcoastbarney

YouTube:

https://www.youtube.com/@barneythewestcoastcockatoo

The Author

Henrietta Kraus was born in Linz in Upper Austria and now lives in the Mödling district near Vienna. She completed a degree in theater studies combined with German studies and literary studies. She also has training in classical singing.

In addition to working in the cultural sector, she dedicated herself to writing, especially children's books, as she enjoyed writing stories for children and young people during her school and university years.

She is a member of the Interest Group of Austrian Authors. Her first book was published in 2016: "Anton vom Mond – Lomi's große Mission" (translated: "Anton from the Moon – Lomi's Great Mission").

More Reading Adventures

Check out our website

www.Leseabenteuer.at

There you will find other exciting books as well as teaching materials to download.

www.ingramcontent.com/pod-product-compliance
Lightning Source LLC
LaVergne TN
LVHW041455190726
843491LV00008B/2379

* 9 7 8 3 9 0 3 2 4 3 6 5 1 *